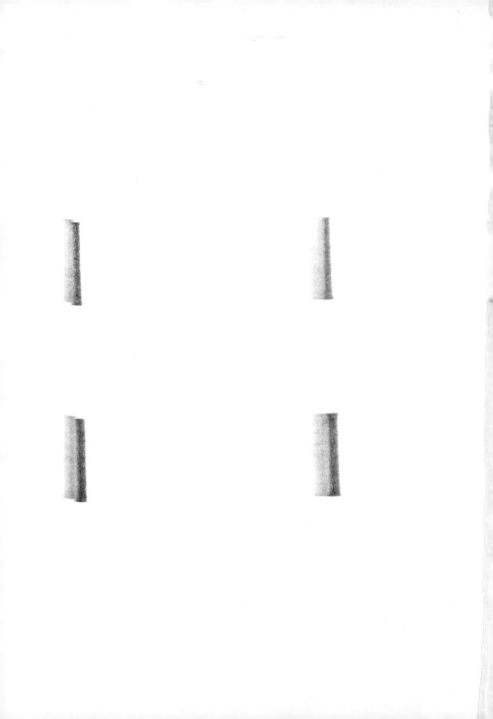

SMOOTH SEA AND A FIGHTING CHANCE

The Story of the Sinking of *Titanic*

BY STEVEN OTFINOSKI

Consultant:
Richard Bell, PhD
Associate Professor of History
University of Maryland, College Park

CAPSTONE PRESS
a capstone imprint

Tangled History is published by Capstone Press,
1710 Roe Crest Drive, North Mankato, Minnesota 56003
www.mycapstone.com

Library of Congress Cataloging-in-Publication Data
Otfinoski, Steven, author.
Smooth sea and a fighting chance : the story of the sinking of Titanic / by Steven
Otfinoski.
pages cm.—(Tangled history)
Summary: "In a narrative nonfiction format, follows people who experienced the
sinking of Titanic"—Provided by publisher.
Includes bibliographical references and index.
ISBN 978-1-4914-8453-1 (library binding)
ISBN 978-1-4914-8457-9 (pbk.)
ISBN 978-1-4914-8461-6 (ebook pdf)
1. Titanic (Steamship)—Juvenile literature. 2. Shipwrecks—North Atlantic Ocean—
Juvenile literature. I. Title.
G530.T6O86 2016
910.9163'4—dc23   2015035084

Editorial Credits
Adrian Vigliano, editor; Heidi Thompson, designer; Tracy Cummins, media researcher;
Laura Manthe, production specialist

Photo Credits
Alamy: Mary Evans Picture Library, cover; Corbis: Bettmann, 11, 57, Daily Mirror/
Mirrorpix, 49 left; Getty Images: Ann Ronan Pictures/Print Collector, 6, Bob Thomas/
Popperfoto, 47, Hulton Archive, 44, 75, Mansell/The LIFE Picture Collection, 24,
ullstein bild/ullstein bild, 23, Universal Images Group, 13, 85, 86; Granger, NYC,
31, 40; Newscom: World History Archive, 4; Shutterstock: Everett Historical, 60;
SuperStock: Illustrated London News Ltd/Mar/Pantheon, 50, 72, 89; The Image
Works: Mary Evans/National Archives, 49 right

Printed in US.
007534CGS16

TABLE OF CONTENTS

FOREWORD

On April 10, 1912, the world's largest and most luxurious ocean liner, the White Star Line's RMS *Titanic*, left Southampton, England, for its maiden voyage to New York.

The *Titanic* was one of the greatest technological wonders the world had ever seen. The ship stretched a massive 882.9 feet (269.1 meters) long and 92.5 feet

(28.2 m) wide. It could reach a top speed of about 24 knots and, with dining rooms, lounges, a squash racquet court, a gymnasium, and a swimming pool, the *Titanic* brought luxury and comfort to a new height in ocean travel. Most strikingly, the ship was equipped with 16 watertight compartments. This safety design would allow the ship to continue floating with up to four of the compartments flooded. This led some people to claim that the *Titanic* was unsinkable.

As it left the dock at Southampton, the *Titanic* nearly collided with another passenger ship, the America Line's SS *New York*. Some superstitious crew members saw this as a bad omen, but others felt they were lucky to avoid an accident. The ship made two brief stops at Cherbourg, France, and Queenstown, Ireland, to take on more passengers. With at least 2,205 passengers and crew members aboard, the *Titanic* headed into the Atlantic Ocean for what promised to be a smooth, five-day sail to New York.

"WE'VE STRUCK AN ICEBERG"

1

Radio operator Cyril Evans had an important message to deliver. Nearly an hour before, his ship, the SS *Californian*, a small British liner bound for Boston, had run into a large field of icebergs in the North Atlantic. Its captain, Stanley Lord, had wisely decided to slow for the night. In the morning the crew would be able to see the icebergs and safely steer around them. Evans was standing on deck with Lord when the captain pointed to a ship's light some distance away.

"Who is she?" Lord asked.

"The *Titanic*," Evans replied. The captain nodded. They knew the huge luxury passenger ship was making its maiden voyage.

"Send her a message to warn her about the icebergs ahead," Lord told the radio operator.

Evans' message was short and to the point: "We are stopped and surrounded by icebergs." But the reply he received from the *Titanic* a few moments later surprised him: "Shut up, shut up, I am busy: I am working ... you are jamming me."

Evans was taken aback by the rudeness of the *Titanic's* radioman. He sounded tired and edgy, but that was no excuse. Evans was tired himself, but had taken the time to deliver the warning. He thought about sending the message again, but didn't want to be told off once more by the man on the other end. So he shut off his radio and prepared to turn in for the night.

John Jacob Astor

First-class suite on the *Titanic*, 11:40 p.m.

A slight jarring of the ship awakened John Jacob Astor IV and his wife, Madeleine. Astor assured Madeleine it was nothing. She was pregnant and needed all the rest she could get.

The thought of a mishap that could delay their arrival in New York irked Astor. As a member of one of the wealthiest families in America, he was used to getting his way. He and Madeleine had left the United States under a cloud more than a year earlier on an extended honeymoon across Europe and Egypt.

When the recently divorced Astor had married the much younger Madeleine, the marriage had created a scandal. Once well respected, Astor had found himself shunned by New York society. He hoped that time had healed the situation and that he and Madeleine would once again be accepted by their peers. Unable to sleep, Astor decided to go out and see just what had happened to the ship.

Margaret Brown

Margaret Brown was reading in bed when the crash came. The ship jolted, throwing her from the brass bed to the deck. She immediately got up, dusted herself off, and decided to investigate.

Brown had been abroad for some time, having toured Egypt with the Astors and her daughter, Helen, who had then returned to her university studies in Paris at the Sorbonne. Margaret Brown's husband, mining millionaire J. J. Brown, was back in Denver, Colorado, seeing to his properties. Mr. Brown wasn't fond of travel.

Margaret Brown kept busy with civic affairs. She had helped establish the first American court for juvenile defendants and was a tireless advocate in the fight for women's suffrage and education. But now she was on a

Margaret Brown

different kind of mission. She put on some clothes and went out into the corridor. There were a number of first-class passengers milling around in their nightclothes, wearing the same puzzled looks on their faces. One gentleman pointed to another in his pajamas and teased, "Are you prepared to swim in those things?" Someone laughed. Then some of them decided to go up on deck to learn more. Brown didn't join them. Instead she went back to her cabin and returned to her book.

Edward Smith

The *Titanic*'s bridge, 11:45 p.m.

Captain Edward Smith knew something was wrong. Several crew members had brought word to him that the ship had grazed an iceberg. That could be serious, but he took some comfort thinking about the ship's watertight compartments that were designed to help in the case of flooding.

Captain Edward Smith

Still, Smith had Fourth Officer Joseph Boxhall inspect the forward part of the ship.

The officer soon returned saying he could find nothing wrong. But Smith didn't rest easy yet. He told Boxhall to get the ship's carpenter, J. Hutchinson, to make a more thorough inspection. But just as he said this, Hutchinson came rushing up to the bridge, out of breath.

"She's taking water fast!" Hutchinson gasped.

J. Bruce Ismay

Aboard the *Titanic*, 11:47 p.m.

When J. Bruce Ismay felt the ship jolt, he took it personally. Ismay was president of the White Star Line, which owned the *Titanic*. Anxious to see what had happened, he threw some clothes over his pajamas, put on his carpet slippers, and headed for the bridge. Captain Smith told him that they had struck an iceberg.

"Do you think the ship is seriously damaged?" Ismay asked.

The captain paused before speaking. "I'm afraid she is," he said.

Harold Bride

The *Titanic*'s radio cabin, 11:50 p.m.

Harold Bride rubbed his eyes, sat up in his bunk, and opened the door that separated his sleeping quarters from the work area. He stared at first operator Jack Phillips, hunched over the radio. The poor man had been sending and receiving messages for hours. Bride, the second operator, wasn't supposed to take over the radio for another two hours, but decided Phillips needed a rest. He put on some clothes and told his partner to get to bed. As devoted as Phillips was to his work, he didn't put up any resistance. But before he turned over the headphones, he gave Bride a stunning piece of news. Phillips said he thought that the ship had run into some kind of trouble. It would probably have to be sent back to Ireland, where it had been built. Bride received the news with mild concern. Even damaged, the *Titanic* would be in little danger. After all, as the newspapers had declared, it was unsinkable.

Edward Smith

The *Titanic*'s bridge, 11:55 p.m.

To find out the full scope of the damage, Captain Smith knew he needed to meet with the one man aboard who could assess the situation accurately—the ship's builder, Thomas Andrews. Smith found Andrews and they made a quick inspection of the ship.

Their inspection revealed that six of the watertight compartments meant to keep the ship afloat had been cut open and water had already flooded them.

Smith swallowed hard as he asked the

critical question, "Can she stay afloat?"

Andrews shook his head. "If up to four compartments had flooded, the ship could stay afloat," he said, "but not six."

Now Smith knew the ship was doomed. *"How much time do we have?" he asked.*

"About an hour to an hour and a half," Andrews replied in a steady voice.

Harold Bride

April 15, 1912, the *Titanic*'s radio cabin, 12:00 a.m.

Bride had no sooner put on his headphones than Captain Smith appeared.

"We've struck an iceberg," he told them. "Get ready to send a call for assistance, but don't send it until I tell you."

With that he was gone. Phillips and Bride stared at each other in shock. Then the captain poked his head in again.

"Send the call for assistance," he said.

Captain Smith faced the grim situation with cool professionalism. After all, he was a 32-year veteran and a senior captain for the White Star Line. With his white beard and regal bearing, Smith was well regarded by both passengers and crew on every ship he sailed. At age 62, he had thought about retirement, but agreed to stay on to sail the *Titanic* on its maiden voyage, something he had done for every White Star liner since 1904.

Smith had never encountered a situation as serious as this, but he knew what was required of him now. He called his officers together on deck. He told them the situation and then gave each his orders. Chief Officer Henry Wilde was to uncover the lifeboats. First Officer William Murdoch was to call out the passengers. Sixth Officer James Moody was to retrieve the list of lifeboat assignments. Smith reminded them that women and children were to be put into the lifeboats first and then men, if there was room left.

Smith thought over the numbers. There were 16 lifeboats. Each could hold up to 65 people. There were also two emergency boats with 40-person capacities and four collapsible boats that could hold 47 people each. That accounted for 1,178 passengers. Unfortunately, there were, including the crew, more than 2,200 people aboard. To save them all he would have to get help from another ship and fast. He prayed that Phillips' distress signals would be quickly answered.

The *Titanic*'s Chief Baker Charles Joughin was off duty when he received the news of the ship's condition and the order to join all other employees on the Boat Deck. But he decided not to obey the order immediately.

At 34 years old Joughin was an experienced sailor, having gone to sea at age 11. He was a loyal crew member, but he also had an independent mind. If the ship was indeed in danger of sinking, he reasoned, people needed more than life belts and lifeboats. They needed food to sustain them until help arrived. He called his crew of 13 bakers and told them to raid the pantry for all the bread they could lay their hands on. He supervised them as they carried the bread, four loaves each, up to the deck.

Second-class passenger Lawrence Beesley had been reading in his bed when the crash came. Peeking into the corridor outside his room, he had asked a passing steward why the ship had stopped.

"I don't know, sir," the steward replied, "but I don't suppose it's anything much."

Discovering nothing on deck, Beesley returned to his book. Beesley had been a science teacher at Dulwich College in Great Britain. Now a widower, he was headed to Toronto, Canada, to visit his brother. His young son remained back in Great Britain.

But now, hearing more commotion above, Beesley decided he could ignore it no longer. He went up to A Deck where some crew members were in the process of loading passengers into lifeboats. It didn't seem to be a serious situation—few women were actually getting into the boats.

Beesley decided to go back to his cabin and wait for a while. But as he descended the stairs, he noticed his feet were not landing on the steps where he intended. The ship seemed to be tilting at a strange angle. When he got back to his room, Beesley decided that, indeed, something was seriously wrong. He put on a warm jacket, stuck some books in the pockets, and immediately returned to A Deck.

Madeleine Astor

First-class suite on the *Titanic*, 12:08 a.m.

Madeleine Astor was relieved to see her husband return.

"We've struck ice, but it isn't serious," he said.

He went on to say it would be a good idea for her to accompany him and the other first-class passengers on the deck. So, to brace herself from the numbing cold outside, Madeleine put on her black coat with the sable trim, a fur muff, and her diamond necklace. She remained calm. In all such important matters, she had complete faith in her husband's judgment.

Madeleine and John Jacob Astor IV

"WOMEN AND CHILDREN FIRST"

2

At first passengers didn't want to board lifeboats, not believing the ship was in any real danger.

Harold Lowe

Aboard the *Titanic*, 12:10 a.m.

Fifth Officer Harold Lowe awoke with a start. He had been sleeping soundly since coming off duty around 8:30 p.m. But a commotion outside his cabin broke through his slumber. Lowe had been with the White Star Line for a little over a year. All the other *Titanic* deck officers knew one another and had worked together on other ships. He felt like the odd man out.

Lowe looked out of his porthole and saw a crowd of people on deck. They were all wearing life belts. Lowe realized something must be terribly wrong with the ship. He quickly dressed, grabbed his revolver, and headed for the deck to do whatever he could to help.

"CQD." Jack Phillips tapped out the letters in Morse code on his Marconi radio. Some operators said the letters stood for "Come Quick, Danger," but in reality the "CQ" was code for "all stations" and the "D" meant emergency. Phillips followed the first code with "MGY," the identification letters for the *Titanic*.

Harold Bride watched from the other side of the cabin as Phillips tapped madly at the radio. "You're really flashing away at that signal," he said with a laugh.

"Can't help it, old man," Phillips replied, returning the laugh. "You know me. All work and no play."

Just then Captain Smith returned. "What are you sending?" he asked Phillips.

"'CQD,'" Phillips replied.

"Send 'SOS,'" Bride suggested. "It's the new call, and it may be your last chance to send it!"

The three men laughed heartily. It may not have changed the seriousness of their situation, Bride thought to himself, but it did relieve some of the stress they were all under.

Cyril Evans

The *Californian*'s radio cabin, 12:15 a.m.

Cyril Evans had no assistant to work alongside him, but he did have a follower of sorts—Third Officer Charles Groves. Evans was still awake when Groves walked into the radio cabin for a chat.

"What ships have you got, Sparks?" he asked eagerly, calling Evans by his nickname.

"Only the *Titanic*," Evans replied, remembering the withering response he had received an hour earlier.

Evans let Groves put on his headphones,

which he often did, but he had already turned off the radio. Groves could have restarted the connection by winding up the magnet sound detector, but Evans didn't tell him this. He was tired and, while he usually looked forward to Groves' visits, he was ready to turn in for the night. So Groves took off the headphones and left, at which point Evans went to bed, deciding that a final check of the radio was unnecessary.

Arthur Rostron

Aboard the *Carpathia*, 12:25 a.m.

Captain Arthur Rostron of the *Carpathia* was resting in his cabin when radio operator Harold Cottam came rushing in. "I've just received a distress signal from the *Titanic*," Cottam said breathlessly.

The news stunned Rostron. He was an experienced veteran of the sea, but had been a ship's captain with the Cunard Line for less than two years. On April 11 he had left New York with the

Carpathia, a small luxury liner carrying about 740 passengers bound for Gibraltar.

"You're positive it's a distress signal and it's from the *Titanic?*" Rostron asked. Cottam nodded vigorously. The captain made his decision quickly. He would turn the ship around and go to the *Titanic's* aid. "Tell him we are coming along as fast as we can," he said to the radio operator. Then he started shooting orders to all his key men.

"Pour on the steam to pick up speed," he told his chief engineer. "And cut off all heat and hot water to divert all steam to the boilers." Next he turned to First Officer H. V. Dean. "Prepare for rescue operations and swing out the lifeboats," he said.

Another crew member questioned if the *Carpathia* was in some kind of trouble. "No, no," Rostron assured him, "we're going to another vessel in distress."

Once the men were at work with their duties, the captain did some quick calculating. The *Titanic* was 58 miles away. Could they get there in time to save all those aboard? Rostron prayed that they would.

Margaret Brown

As she made her way up to A Deck, Margaret Brown recalled a conversation she had had with her new friend Emma Bucknell soon after they boarded the ship at Cherbourg, France. Bucknell had said, "I have a premonition about this ship."

"Nonsense," replied Brown, "you're just anxious to get home and see your family." Now she wondered if Bucknell could truly see into the future.

Before reaching A Deck, she saw the crew trying to release the lifeboats in order to lower them. She was appalled at their lack of skill. They demonstrated none of the discipline and professionalism she had witnessed on board German ocean liners where the lifeboat drills were conducted with military precision. She shook her head, truly wondering if the *Titanic's* crew had ever done this before.

Now on A Deck, she spotted Bucknell nearby in the crowd while strapping on her life belt. When she looked up, Bucknell drew close and whispered, "Didn't I tell you something was going to happen?"

Charles Joughin

After a brief stop in his cabin, baker Joughin
was ready to return to work. He went directly
to Lifeboat No. 10, the one he was appointed to
load and skipper. While "women and children
first" was the tradition, the captain required that
each boat have at least two able-bodied seamen
from the crew to navigate it.

The problem, Joughin could clearly see, was
that most women were extremely reluctant to
get into the lifeboats. Many didn't want to leave
their husbands and other male family members.
Others felt it was too risky to get into the fragile
lifeboats that were to be lowered some 50 feet
down to the chilly, churning ocean waters below.
They preferred to stay on a ship that still seemed
secure and stable.

Other officers seemed to be doing their best
to persuade reluctant women to climb in, but

Joughin thought a more direct approach was needed. He began grabbing women and children from the A Deck, taking them to the Boat Deck, and forcing them into Lifeboat No. 10. This method seemed to work.

By 1:20 a.m. Joughin had loaded about 30 passengers onto the lifeboat. Although the boat was less than half full, Joughin decided it was time to launch. While making preparations to launch, he realized that there were three other crew members in the boat. Joughin didn't think they needed a fourth man aboard. He decided that going with the boat would set a bad example for other able-bodied men, so he helped lower it down into the ocean.

Leah Aks

Eighteen-year-old Leah Aks was determined to board a lifeboat. She, along with her 10-month-old son, Frank Phillip, was on her way to join her husband in Norfolk, Virginia. Born in Warsaw, Poland, she had been living in London with her family when she met and married tailor Samuel Aks. Work was hard to find in London, and when a cousin invited him to try his luck in America, Samuel went. He saved up enough money to send to Leah for her passage. She was scheduled to leave on another ship, but her mother told her to take the *Titanic*, which she felt was safer. Aks and "Filly," as she called her baby, came on board in Southampton, Great Britain, as third-class passengers. Although accommodations for third class were often sparse and crowded, third class on the *Titanic* was underbooked. Aks felt fortunate to get a private cabin.

Now the "safe" ship was in danger of sinking. About a half hour earlier, Aks had joined other third-class passengers at the foot of the staircase in the ship's rear. Finally crew members told the women and children to come up to the Boat Deck to board lifeboats. Aks held Filly in her arms as she tried to make her way up the staircase. Some women were carried bodily to the deck by crew members. Soon, Aks found herself being carried too, with Filly still in her arms.

It was extremely cold on the Boat Deck and Filly shivered. A well-dressed young woman wearing a diamond necklace took off her shawl and covered Filly's head with it. Aks thanked her and the woman moved away with her husband.

J. Bruce Ismay

As head of the White Star Line, J. Bruce Ismay felt it was his duty to help direct the loading and lowering of the lifeboats. He could see that some members of the crew didn't appreciate his help. He'd caught a few of the men casting cold stares at the carpet slippers on his feet. But this didn't deter him. Ismay waved his arms and told Officer Lowe to lower his boat faster.

Lowe whirled around and shouted, "Do you want me to lower away quickly? You'll have me drown the whole lot of them!"

Ismay was taken aback by Lowe's outburst and crept away to the rear.

John Jacob Astor

The *Titanic's* A Deck, 12:45 a.m.

By the time they reached A Deck, John Jacob Astor knew the seriousness of their situation. He had run into Captain Smith on the staircase and Smith told Astor the grave danger they were in. Astor had swallowed hard, kept a calm demeanor, and returned to his group. "You'd better all put your life belts on," he told them.

While the other wealthy men and women chatted among themselves, Astor took his wife into the ship's gymnasium. They sat side by side.

"You're shivering, Madeleine," he said. "You never should have given that woman your shawl."

"Her baby needed it more than I did, John," she replied.

He sighed and tried to explain the crisis to her in terms that would not unduly upset her.

She questioned the necessity of the life belt, asking if it would actually help if she found herself in the water. To assure her, Astor took a penknife from his pocket and sliced open an extra life belt. Out spilled tiny pieces of cork. He told her the cork would help them float. This seemed to make her feel better, at least for the moment.

Edward Smith

The *Titanic*'s bridge, 12:45 a.m.

So far, the *Carpathia* was the only ship that seemed to understand the seriousness of the *Titanic*'s situation. But Captain Smith knew that despite the best efforts of the *Carpathia*'s crew, it might not arrive in time to help the *Titanic*. He needed to alert closer ships. Frustratingly, the ship that appeared to be only 10 miles away remained motionless despite Phillips' distress messages. Deciding it was time to take more drastic steps, he had Quartermaster George Rowe prepare rockets on the bridge. "Fire one, and fire one every five or six minutes," he told Rowe.

The first rocket shot into the night sky like a firework, bursting into a shower of stars that rained down on the water below. From the bridge the captain could see passengers looking up in awe and then murmuring darkly to one another. He knew that the desperateness of their situation must finally be sinking in for many of them. Surely everyone knew the meaning of rockets at sea.

Herbert Stone

Aboard the *Californian*, 12:50 a.m.

While most of the *Californian's* crew was asleep, Second Officer Herbert Stone was awake and on watch. From the bridge he saw a distant rocket blaze in the night sky. He stared across the dark ocean as another rocket shot toward the stars. *It must be a ship in communication with some other ship*, he thought, *or possibly a signal to us to tell us they have big icebergs around them.* He went about his business, planning to inform the captain at the first opportunity.

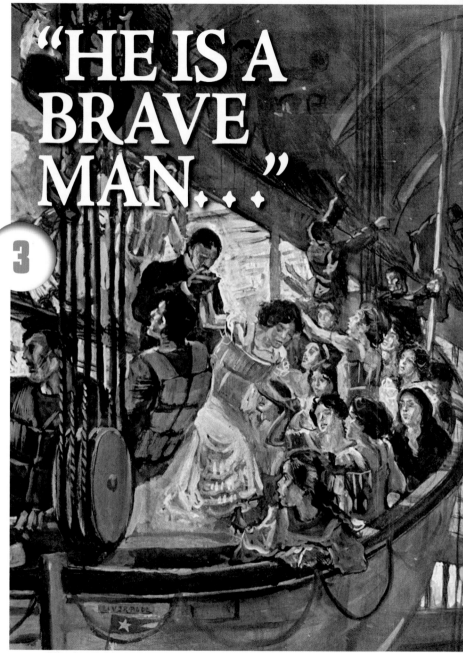

"HE IS A BRAVE MAN..."

3

The first lifeboat launched with only 28 people on board despite being equipped to carry 65 passengers.

Margaret Brown

The *Titanic*'s A Deck, 12:50 a.m.

Margaret Brown watched as her concerns about the boarding of the lifeboats proved all too true. In their rush to get the women and children into the boats and onto the water, the crew members were sending off boats that were only partly filled.

Brown decided to investigate the starboard side of the ship, but before she could, two crew members grabbed her and said, "you are going, too." Then they pushed her into Lifeboat No. 6 just as it started its descent. Brown counted 28 passengers and crew around her. She shook her head, estimating that this was little more than a third of the people the boat could carry.

Jack Thayer

Seventeen-year-old Jack Thayer
followed his parents and his mother's maid
up onto A Deck amid a pressing crowd
of other passengers. His father, John
Borland Thayer, was a vice president of
the Pennsylvania Railroad and one of the
many millionaires aboard the *Titanic*. Upon
reaching A Deck, the foursome parted at
the top of the grand staircase. Jack said
good-bye to his mother, Marian, and her
maid, as they headed for the lifeboats on the
ship's port side. Jack followed his father to
the starboard side, where they hoped to find
a lifeboat that would take men.

They had only been separated for
a short time, however, when a steward
informed them that Mrs. Thayer was still
on board the ship. The family reunited and

they headed off to find another lifeboat.

The crowds on deck were now huge, and Jack got separated from his parents. He was not, however, alone. Tagging along with the Thayers was 29-year-old Milton Long, whom Jack had befriended that evening after dinner. Long, the son of a Springfield, Massachusetts, judge, was traveling alone on the *Titanic*. Long and Jack decided to stick together until they could locate Jack's parents. But as the moments passed and the ship's listing grew worse, that prospect seemed less and less probable.

Arthur Rostron

Aboard the *Carpathia*, 1:05 a.m.

The *Carpathia* was humming with activity. Under Captain Rostron's orders, the ship's surgeon, Dr. Frank McGhee, had set up first-aid stations in each of the three dining saloons. Meanwhile, the ship's chief purser and steward were placing crew members at each gangway to receive the survivors of the *Titanic*. Once in the saloons, the survivors would find blankets, hot coffee, tea, and soup.

Rostron gave his crew strict orders to say nothing about these preparations to the *Carpathia*'s passengers, many of whom were still asleep in their cabins. The captain knew he and his men had a difficult task ahead, and he wanted no civilians getting in their way.

Captain Arthur Rostron

Margaret Brown

Margaret Brown was not happy. By her count, six lifeboats had been launched on the sea, and she would have preferred to be aboard any one of them rather than the one in which she now sat.

The commander of Lifeboat No. 6 was Quartermaster Robert Hichens, a man in whose leadership skills Brown had little faith. Instead of instilling confidence and calm in the others, Hichens seemed nervous and afraid. He even predicted that they would never safely reach land or a rescue ship. *He's shivering like an aspen tree!* Brown thought, watching Hitchens.

Brown and another woman took the oars and rowed as Hichens tried to guide the boat. "Faster! Faster!" he cried at the rowers.

"If you don't make better speed with your rowing we'll be pulled down to our deaths!"

He pointed to the *Titanic*, which was sinking lower and lower into the sea. "If you don't move this boat faster we'll be sucked down to the bottom of the sea with her!" Brown gritted her teeth and continued to pull on her oar.

Harold Lowe
Aboard Lifeboat No. 14, 1:25 a.m.

Since 12:45 a.m. seven lifeboats had been launched, and Officer Lowe had helped lower several of them. He tried to strike a balance of firm discipline and courtesy, but it wasn't easy. When two angry men jumped into Lifeboat No. 14, he pulled out his pistol and fired several times into the air. They got the message and fell back.

Lowe made his final preparations to leave *Titanic* and command Lifeboat No. 14. Now, with a load of 63 people, Lowe gave the order to lower the boat. He kept his pistol close, firing warning shots as they passed each deck. He couldn't risk any desperate people trying to jump from the decks into the boat.

It wasn't easy to leave when there were hundreds still in need of assistance, but he couldn't let the boatful of women and children go down to the waters with no one to safely navigate the vessel. He would follow the captain's orders to the letter—staying close to the other boats and heading for the distant light that they hoped was a rescue ship. He knew their lives depended on it.

Harold Bride

Jack Phillips was frustrated. After an hour of messages, one ship, the *Frankfurt*, still didn't understand the *Titanic*'s desperation. So Phillips kept at it, tapping away madly at the keyboard. Harold Bride's admiration for Phillips grew constantly. He only wished he could do more to help.

With Phillips glued to his post, Bride regularly went out to see what was happening on deck and brought reports back to the radio cabin. Captain Smith also dropped in on them several times with news, most of it grim. One time he warned them the power might soon be lost, as the water had now reached the engine room.

Phillips didn't seem concerned and continued with his relentless messaging.

He is a brave man, Bride thought, *sticking to his work while everyone else is raging about.*

Jack Phillips

Harold Bride

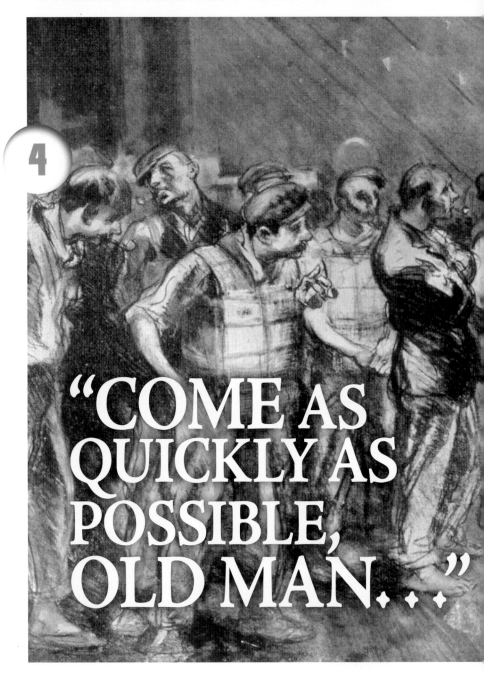

4

"COME AS QUICKLY AS POSSIBLE, OLD MAN…"

Leah Aks

Leah Aks waited patiently in line despite the cold, holding Filly close. It had been over an hour since she reached the deck from the third-class cabins. Finally she could see people starting to board Lifeboat No. 13 and knew her turn would come soon.

Suddenly there was a disturbance in the crowd. Aks could see that a man who had tried to get into the lifeboat was now being pulled back by crew members. One of the crew members spoke above the confusion, "Women and children are to board first!"

Pushing his way through the crowd, the man who had tried to board the boat came face-to-face with Aks. His wild, desperate eyes fell on the baby in her arms. "I'll show you women and children first!" he cried, seizing Filly from her grip and heaving him over the side of the ship.

Aks screamed as the man disappeared into the crowd. She rushed to the rail, but before she could reach it she felt hands grabbing her. She struggled desperately against the crew members who held her, but it was no use. Moments later the men pushed her into Lifeboat No. 13.

Aks collapsed in the boat, crying. Through her tears she saw that many other women were weeping. She thought of Filly as she cried out into the cold night.

Lawrence Beesley

Aboard Lifeboat No. 13, 1:40 a.m.

Lawrence Beesley felt lucky to find a place in Lifeboat No. 13. He was thrilled when he realized that the boat's officer was welcoming men to fill up the empty seats. But he felt much less lucky when the lifeboat was nearly flooded and overturned on the way down to the water. As crew members lowered the boat by ropes, the craft neared a drainage pipe on the *Titanic's* side. Huge amounts of water gushed from the hole. As the lifeboat drew closer to the dangerous flow, Beesley and others shouted desperately to the crew above. To their great relief, the crew was able to manipulate the ropes and move the lifeboat out of the path of the rushing water.

But their problems weren't over. When the lifeboat finally reached the water, they had difficulty cutting the ropes that attached the boat to the ship. They drifted a short distance until they were directly below Lifeboat No. 15, which was just starting its descent. Again, the lifeboat passengers cried up to the crew. But No. 15 did not stop its descent. Luckily they were able to cut No. 13 loose and float away just in time.

Beesley breathed a deep sigh of relief. He looked up at the clear sky, then down at the dark, calm waters. It would have been a beautiful scene, if not for the huge ship slowly sinking only a short distance away.

J. Bruce Ismay

J. Bruce Ismay continued to help load the lifeboats after being rebuffed by Officer Lowe, but he tried not to attract too much attention. Now his work was near its end. Almost all the lifeboats had been launched and only a few remained. Among them was Collapsible C, the only one of the four emergency boats that was easily accessible to the deck.

Ismay noticed that the boat, occupied mostly by women and children, still had space. The director of the White Star Line did not want to go down with the ship. He believed he had done what he could to help others and now it was time to help himself. And why shouldn't he? Looking around to see if anyone was watching, he stepped over the rail and took a seat in the lifeboat.

John Jacob Astor

John Jacob Astor led his wife over stacks of deck chairs to Lifeboat No. 4. The boat could only be accessed by passing through the open windows of the deck's promenade with the deck chairs serving as steps. Helping Madeleine into the boat, Astor asked an officer if he could join his wife in the boat due to her delicate condition.

"No sir. No men are allowed in these boats until the women are loaded first," the officer replied.

Astor turned to reassure a distraught Madeleine. "The sea's calm," he said. "You'll be all right. You're in good hands." Then, after a moment, he added, "I'll meet you in the morning." He handed her his gloves, turned back to the ship, and watched No. 4, the last of the lifeboats, begin its descent to the sea, half empty.

Harold Bride

Both Bride and Phillips were now pinning all their hopes on the *Carpathia*.

"Come as quickly as possible, old man; the engine room is filling up to the boilers," Phillips tapped to the *Carpathia*.

Bride did what he could to make his partner comfortable at his post. He put his overcoat on his shoulders and strapped a life belt on him. Bride was surprised when Phillips let him take over the radio while he went out on deck to see what was going on. Phillips came back a short time later, shaking his head. "Things look very queer," he said.

In this reenactment, the *Carpathia*'s radio operator exchanges messages with the *Titanic*.

Jack Thayer

The *Titanic*'s Boat Deck, 1:49 a.m.

Jack Thayer's efforts to find his parents had failed. He could only hope that they were both safely off the ship and on a lifeboat. He still, however, had Milton Long, his newfound friend, for company. They exchanged messages to give one another's family if one made it off the ship alive and the other didn't.

The lifeboats were all gone now. Thayer and Long watched as a number of desperate people jumped overboard.

"Let's jump," Thayer said. "We can swim to one of the lifeboats."

Long disagreed. "We'll drown for sure. Let's stay on the ship."

As they continued to argue the issue, Thayer couldn't help noticing that the *Titanic* was sinking lower and lower into the dark waves.

Charles Joughin

Feeling rather unsteady, baker Joughin made his way to B Deck. The tilt of the ship was growing worse by the minute and making walking difficult.

Joughin tried to focus on what he could do to help. Seeing passengers in the water trying to swim to the departing lifeboats, he decided to lend a hand. He began hurling deck chairs through the open windows and into the sea. He hoped that struggling swimmers would find and cling to the floating chairs.

On deck, people stood watching but no one joined him in his mission. After tossing some 50 chairs overboard, Joughin went back to the pantry on A Deck to get something to drink. All he could find was water.

"NOW IT'S EVERY MAN FOR HIMSELF"

5

From his seat in the lifeboat, Lawrence Beesley could see that *Titanic* couldn't last much longer. The ship reminded him of a stricken animal as it sank lower and lower in the sea. A strange stillness fell over the crowded lifeboat.

Near Beesley sat three Swedish girls, staying close together for warmth in the frigid night air. Next to him sat a woman with a small baby boy in her arms. She asked if he would check to see if the baby's feet were uncovered. He found they were and tucked the blanket under the baby's feet. The woman with the baby sounded strangely familiar. Beesley suddenly realized they had become acquainted on the ship. Now they were among a small group of passengers on a much smaller vessel.

Leah Aks

It was obvious that many of the women on board Lifeboat No. 13 were anxious about the uncertain fate of their men still on the *Titanic*. Leah Aks didn't know if her child was alive or dead. With her own eyes she had seen Filly tossed overboard by a madman. She couldn't bring herself to care about the *Titanic's* final fate or the possibility of rescue.

She sat in the boat completely isolated, feeling numb to the world.

Captain Smith had largely played a supportive role in the last two hours, encouraging proper boarding of the lifeboats and trying to maintain a stable presence. Now, with only a short time left before the ship sank under the waves, he went about his final duties. One of his first stops was the radio cabin.

"Men," he told Phillips and Bride, "you have done your full duty. You can do no more. Abandon your cabin. Now it's every man for himself." The two men did not stir from their chairs. "You look out for yourselves," Smith said quietly. "I release you. That's the way of it at this kind of time…"

Smith could see that neither man was ready to give up signaling for help. He decided there was nothing more he could say, so he left them to their work and continued his last rounds.

Charles Joughin

Baker Joughin came up once more onto the port side of A Deck. The ship was listing so badly that he and everyone else on the deck were having difficulty standing upright. A large crowd was rushing from the Boat Deck and he followed them. The ship's stern had risen high into the air. The *Titanic* now seemed nearly perpendicular in the water.

Many people were thrust against the port rail, but Joughin managed to stay on his feet. Then the moving ship forced him over the starboard rail, and he suddenly found himself standing on the side of the vessel. He slid down the side, trying to hold on.

Adjusting his life belt, Joughin suddenly felt the ship drop down into the sea. It was as if he were rapidly riding down in an elevator. As he reached the waterline, the baker slipped off into the water. It was shockingly cold. He shivered and began to paddle away from the ship, keeping his head above the water.

Jack Thayer
The *Titanic*'s Boat Deck, 2:10 a.m.

Jack Thayer had finally convinced Milton Long that the only way they could save themselves was to jump overboard. The two young men shook hands and wished each other all the best. Then they both jumped up on the rail. "You are coming, boy, aren't you?" Long asked.

"Go ahead," Thayer replied. "I'll be with you in a minute."

Long slid down the side of the ship. Thayer took a deep breath and leaped out as far as he could from the ship. He hit the frigid water and his body began shaking at the shock. He swam toward the nearest lifeboats, about 500 yards away.

After a difficult swim, he made it to an overturned lifeboat. Some of the men balancing on the boat pulled him from the water. Once aboard he looked frantically for his friend. But there was no sign of Long in the dark waters.

John Jacob Astor

The *Titanic*'s Boat Deck, 2:12 a.m.

John Jacob Astor could have joined the ever-growing group of first-class passengers near him on the deck. With few options left to them, these men were preparing to go down with the ship as gentlemen. But Astor preferred his own company at this difficult time. His thoughts were with Madeleine, safe aboard the lifeboat and carrying his child. He realized now that he would probably not live to see his baby's birth.

Harold Bride

Returning to the cabin from another tour of the deck, Harold Bride found a lady who had been brought in by her husband in a state of shock. Bride fetched her a glass of water and she revived enough to be taken out by her grateful husband. To Bride's surprise Phillips seemed oblivious to this incident. He continued tapping out messages and waiting for word from the *Carpathia*.

Bride shook his head and went to their sleeping quarters to gather up money. When he returned he found another visitor, this one most unwelcome. It was one of the ship's stokers. He was attempting to unfasten Phillips' life belt.

"Get your hands off him!" Bride cried. He jumped on the stoker and wrestled him to the floor. Finally taking notice, Phillips turned and threw himself into the fight.

"Hold on to him, Harold," said Phillips, punching the invader as he struggled in Bride's grip. Soon the man lost consciousness. The two radio operators looked at one another. Bride knew the time had come to go.

"Come on, let's clear out!" Phillips said.

All was chaos as the two radio operaters emerged on deck. People were leaping off the rails while others stood frozen, not sure what to do. A nearby group of well-dressed gentlemen seemed to be facing the end quietly. But a few had not given up hope. Two lifeboats, Collapsible A and B, were attached to the roof of the officers' quarters. A group of men worked desperately to free the boats from the roof. Bride rushed to join them.

As they struggled, a giant wave washed up on deck and Collapsible A floated off the ship freely. Moments later Bride held onto an oarlock as Collapsible B was washed away from the *Titanic* with about a dozen men aboard. From the icy waters he looked up and saw the huge ship standing straight up against the starry sky. *It looks like a duck ready to go down for a dive,* he thought.

A tremendous crash came from the *Titanic* and echoed across the frigid waters. Margaret Brown stopped rowing and looked up just in time to see the ship go down. She watched in awe as the sea opened up and the surface foamed like giant arms. Dark waves spread around the ship, and the vessel disappeared from sight. In the moments after the ship went under, Brown gazed around her. Everything seems strangely quiet, she thought.

Lawrence Beesley

Aboard Lifeboat No. 13, 2:20 a.m.

As Lawrence Beesley looked on, the *Titanic*'s lights went out and then came back on for an instant before going out again. Then he heard a tremendous noise from the ship as it stood nearly straight up in the water. It was as if, he thought, all the heavy things one could think of had been thrown downstairs from the top of a house, smashing each other and the stairs and everything in the way. Several minutes passed and the ship remained perpendicular, seemingly suspended in time. Then, as he watched, the sea closed over the ship and he knew he had seen the last of the *Titanic*.

Arthur Rostron

Captain Rostron stood on the bridge, searching the darkness ahead for signs of the *Titanic*. The *Carpathia* was speeding along at 17.5 knots, a record high speed for the vessel. He prayed they would make it in time.

Dr. McGhee arrived to report that all preparations had been completed for the arrival of the survivors. Soon after, Rostron saw something on the dark horizon—a green light. "There's his light!" he cried. "He must still be afloat!"

He took a deep breath, hoping they would reach the *Titanic* in time.

"WE HAVE A SMOOTH SEA AND A FIGHTING CHANCE"

6

Harold Lowe

Now that the *Titanic* was gone, Fifth Officer Lowe felt determined not to lose any of the remaining vessels—the lifeboats. He herded boats No. 10, No. 12, No. 4, and Collapsible D together and tied them to his, No. 14. All of the others had fewer people aboard than No. 14, so Lowe divided his 55 passengers among them.

Lowe planned to go back to find survivors at the wreckage site and he needed the strongest team of oarsmen to do it. The cries of swimmers in the water could now be heard echoing clearly across the cold night wind. As soon as the passengers were settled in their new boats and he had his team of oarsmen, Lowe set off on his rescue mission.

Harold Bride

Aboard Collapsible B, 2:35 a.m.

Harold Bride had been swept into the sea with Collapsible B. The only trouble was that the boat had flipped over in its fall and he was now underneath it. Hearing voices above, Bride managed to struggle out and grab onto the boat's upturned bottom. About two dozen other men had the same idea. Most of them managed to pull themselves up onto the boat and stand on it with some difficulty.

An officer whom Bride recognized as Charles Lightoller quickly took command of the boat. He had the men stand in two rows, one on each side of the center. When the water swayed the boat, Lightoller called out for them to lean to the right or left. This kept the vessel stable, but as more men climbed aboard, the boat sank deeper into the sea. The water eventually rose to the passengers' knees.

Minutes passed, then hours. Bride did his best to stay strong and help with this precarious balancing act. Every so often a man gave in to cold and exhaustion and slipped off into the dark waters.

It was clear that there were hundreds of survivors in the water. Sitting in Lifeboat No. 13, Lawrence Beesley could hear their plaintive cries for help. He, along with many others, wanted to return to save lives, but their boat was filled to capacity and had no room. So they followed the command of their leader, one of the stokers, and rowed away from the voices. A few people began to sing to take their minds off the dead and dying. Beesley and others joined them, but they soon fell silent. Beesley found he had no heart for singing and neither, it seemed, did the others.

Margaret Brown

Margaret Brown wanted to go back to find survivors, but Quartermaster Hichens wouldn't hear of it. He said he was still convinced they would be sucked down by the sinking *Titanic* or capsized by swimmers trying to climb aboard their lifeboat. Brown doubted either would happen. The ship had already disappeared from view. And as for the poor people in the water, they probably had little energy left to do anything but float. However, Brown could see Hichens would not change his mind, so she reluctantly accepted his decision not to turn back.

"There's no rescue ship in sight," Hichens raved. "I tell you we're doomed."

This was the last straw for Brown. "Keep it to yourself if you feel that way," she told him. "For the sake of these women and children, be a man. *We have a smooth sea and a fighting chance.*"

She returned to her oar, pulling at it harder than ever. She hoped they would soon spot a rescue ship and prove Hichens and his dire predictions wrong.

Arthur Rostron

Aboard the *Carpathia*, 3:30 a.m.

Closer and closer the *Carpathia* drew to the position of the *Titanic* and still Captain Rostron saw no sign of the stricken ship. What he did see were icebergs, large and small, all around them. He skillfully maneuvered past each obstacle, careful to keep his ship from suffering the same fate as the *Titanic*. He ordered rockets to be set off every 15 minutes and between them, Roman candle fireworks. If the *Titanic* were still afloat, at least its passengers would know help was on the way.

Both crew and passengers were now ready and

waiting for the survivors. The chilly air was filled with excitement. A routine voyage to Gibraltar had turned into a grand adventure of rescue.

"The old boat is as excited as any of us," Rostron overheard a nearby sailor say.

Cyril Evans

Aboard the *Californian*, 3:35 a.m.

Radio operator Cyril Evans was rudely awakened from a sound sleep by Chief Officer George Stewart. "There is a ship that has been firing rockets in the night," Stewart told him. "Please see if there is anything the matter."

Rubbing his eyes, Evans slipped on his headphones. He picked up a message from another liner, the *Frankfurt*, saying that the *Titanic* had struck an iceberg and was sinking. Aghast, Evans told Stewart the grim news and the officer rushed off to find Captain Lord.

Officer Lowe's rescue mission had proved all but fruitless. In nearly an hour, he and his men had picked up only three survivors from the water. These included a steward and first-class passenger W. F. Hoyt, who was not doing well. Lowe knew that in these frigid North Atlantic waters, a swimmer could only hope to survive 20 to 30 minutes before hypothermia set in. They had discovered mostly floating corpses, buoyed by their life belts.

Now they came upon a passenger who had used a rope to lash himself to a door. He floated face down and made no response to Lowe's cries. Thinking the man dead, Lowe turned the boat around. But something made him go back one more time. They lifted the man aboard and the passengers in the boat frantically rubbed his chest, hands, and feet.

Suddenly he opened his eyes, stretched out his arms, and began to speak in his native tongue—Lowe thought he might be Chinese.

A few minutes later the rescued man shocked Lowe, taking an oar from an exhausted sailor and rowing as if his life depended on it.

Charles Joughin
Alongside Collapsible B, 4:00 a.m.

Baker Joughin didn't know what helped him stay alive in the freezing waters for more than two hours. He guessed it was his hearty constitution, or perhaps it was just dumb luck. But it didn't matter. He was alive, paddling, and treading water. He refused to be intimidated by the ocean. It's just like a pond, he thought.

Finally he sighted what he thought was wreckage and swam toward it. It turned out to be an upside-down boat. Joughin stared up in wonder at the men standing perfectly still on the bottom. There was no room for him.

Joughin paddled to the other side of the boat and there he spotted a familiar face, cook Isaac Maynard. Maynard saw him as well and held out a hand. Joughin grasped it. And so he was towed behind, his body still submerged in the icy water. He wasn't about to complain.

Arthur Rostron

Aboard the *Carpathia*, 4:00 a.m.

Captain Rostron brought his ship to a halt. They had reached the spot where the *Titanic* should be and there was nothing but sea. For all their efforts, it had come to this. They must be too late. Then a crew member cried out. He saw something in the darkness. It was a lifeboat, filled with people. It was only a few hundred yards away. Rostron gave the order to start up the engines.

Margaret Brown hated to admit it but she was beginning to think that Hichens' pessimism was warranted. They had been rowing aimlessly for hours with no vessels in sight except for the other lifeboats. Suddenly a woman cried out, "There is a flash of lightning!"

They all looked, including Hichens, who muttered, "It is a falling star."

But it was a ship—Brown was sure of it. She guessed it was at least six or seven miles away, but they could see other lifeboats heading in its direction. Hichens gave the order to start rowing again. For once, Margaret Brown didn't argue with him.

Arthur Rostron

"Stop your engines!" cried a voice out of the darkness. Captain Rostron ordered lines dropped and in moments the first *Titanic* survivor, a woman, was climbing up a rope ladder into the arms of purser Ernest Brown.

When all the passengers from the lifeboat were aboard, Rostron had the officer in command of the lifeboat, Joseph Boxhall, come to the bridge. The captain knew the answer to his question, but he had to ask it anyway. "The *Titanic* has gone down?" he said.

"Yes," Boxhall replied, his voice breaking with emotion, "she went down about 2:30 a.m."

In the half-light of dawn, Rostron looked out from the bridge. He could now see a number of other lifeboats surrounding them amid a field of icebergs.

"WHERE'S DADDY?"

7

J. Bruce Ismay

The director of the White Star Line stumbled up the ladder that connected Collapsible C to the *Carpathia*. Trembling and dazed in his overcoat and pajamas, he felt himself repeating over and over again, "I'm Ismay … I'm Ismay," to no one in particular.

He followed the kindly Dr. McGhee to the dining saloon, but when the doctor offered him something to drink, Ismay refused. "No, I really don't want anything at all," he said. "Could you take me to some room where I can be quiet?"

McGhee led Ismay to the doctor's own cabin, where Ismay collapsed on a bunk bed. Thoughts of shame and guilt swirled through his head. He had survived when so many others had stayed on the ship and perished. After a time, exhaustion overcame him and he found peace in a deep sleep.

Jack Thayer was among the survivors of the last lifeboat to be rescued. Neither he nor the others on No. 12 had an easy time boarding the *Carpathia*. Rough seas prevented the lifeboat from moving close enough to the ship for the passengers to climb up the rope ladder. Instead, crew members threw out a rope with a wooden board on the bottom. When it was Thayer's turn, he sat on the board as if it were a swing and held on tight to the thick rope as he was hoisted up. When he was within reach, a dozen crew members pulled him aboard the *Carpathia*. Out of the sea of faces on deck he saw his mother emerge and rushed to her arms.

"Where's Daddy?" she asked.

Thayer stared at her blankly. "I don't know, Mother," he said.

The *Carpathia* rescued about 705 *Titanic* survivors.

Margaret Brown

The *Carpathia*'s dining saloon, 8:45 a.m.

Margaret Brown made her way to the dining saloon. The saloon was filled with survivors resting, drinking, and eating. Suddenly, amid the din of voices, she saw Quartermaster Robert Hichens.

Brown watched as Hichens jabbered away to anyone who would listen about his heroic efforts to bring his lifeboat to safety. She saw some other passengers who had been in the lifeboat casting hard looks in Hichens' direction. Eventually Brown entered his field of vision and scowled. She must have caught his eye, because he did not continue telling his tales, but made a hasty retreat.

Stanley Lord

Aboard the *Californian*, 9:00 a.m.

Captain Lord received official news of the *Titanic's* fate by semaphore signals from the *Carpathia* at 8:00 a.m. Captain Rostron sent messages asking if the *Californian* would search the site for lifeboats from the *Titanic*.

Captain Lord was more than willing to oblige. But after an hour's search, they found no bodies. Lord gave the order to continue on to Boston.

Her rescue by the *Carpathia* meant little to Leah Aks. Again and again she relived in her mind the horrible moment when that madman had taken Filly. To try to take her mind off the tragedy, a friend invited her to go for a walk on the deck. Aks reluctantly agreed.

While walking they passed another survivor—a woman with a baby in her arms. Aks stopped suddenly, her face pale.

"What's the matter?" her friend asked.

"That ... that's my Filly!" she sputtered. Before her companion could respond, Aks rushed up to the woman holding her child. "You have my baby!" Aks cried.

The woman look back with surprise, then her eyes narrowed. "This baby is mine!" she said fiercely. "God dropped him into my arms!"

Aks couldn't believe what she was hearing. Has everyone gone mad? she thought. "It's my baby," she insisted. "And I want him back."

With that, she moved to take him, but the woman pulled away from her. Clutching Filly to her breast, this stranger ran away down the deck. Aks tried to follow, but her friend seized her by the arm. "No," she said. "Let's go tell the captain. He'll get your baby back."

Harold Bride

Aboard the *Carpathia*, 10:45 a.m.

Harold Bride reclined in a bunk, trying to recover from his ordeal. He had fainted while trying to board the *Carpathia* and had to be carried aboard. Suddenly he heard a knock on the door. It was Captain Rostron. "How are you feeling?" Rostron asked.

"Much better now, thank you, Captain," Bride replied.

"Glad to hear it," said Rostron. He began explaining that their only radio operator, Thomas Cottam, was overwhelmed and exhausted. It seemed like every survivor had messages to send to friends and family on shore to let them know he or she was alive and well. "Do you feel well enough to go back to work?" the captain asked. "If you could lend a hand in the radio cabin it would be an immense help."

Bride smiled. "I'd be happy to help out," he said. "Tom and I are old friends."

So, in a short time, Bride was sitting at the radio table, sending out messages of comfort and hope. Bride knew if Jack Phillips were still alive he'd be proud.

Arthur Rostron
Captain's cabin aboard the *Carpathia*, 11:15 a.m.

Captain Rostron looked at the two women seated before him and then at the baby lying on his bunk. Each woman insisted that the baby was hers and that the other woman was a liar. One of them, he reasoned, must be telling the truth. But which one?

He calmly asked if either woman could provide proof that the child was hers.

They stared at him saying nothing. He continued. "Is there anything on the child's body, a mark, perhaps, that you can describe to me?"

Suddenly, one woman's eyes lit up. "Yes!" she cried. "On his chest there is a birthmark!" She proceeded to describe it in detail. The captain examined the baby. The birthmark was there.

The other woman, an Italian who spoke broken English, refused to accept this. She cried that God had given her the baby as a gift to make up for the loss of her husband on the *Titanic*.

The woman, who said her name was Leah Aks, explained that the Italian had been in a lifeboat and caught her child when a man threw him overboard. Rostron sighed. He lifted the child from the bunk. "Can you nurse it?" he asked the Italian woman.

The woman took the child and held it to her breast. But, although she was pregnant, the infant would not feed.

"Your turn," Rostron said, holding out the baby to Aks. The woman unbuttoned her blouse and held the baby to her breast. He began to drink almost instantly.

"Madame," the captain said, "your child has been returned to you."

April 16, 1912, Dr. McGhee's cabin aboard
the *Carpathia*, 12:00 p.m.

Jack Thayer was surprised when Dr. McGhee
asked if he'd pay a visit to J. Bruce Ismay. "The
poor man hasn't left my cabin since he came
aboard," Dr. McGhee explained. "He spends
every waking moment writing feverish radio
messages to the White Star Line. He hasn't
eaten anything but an occasional bowl of soup.
The man's in bad shape."

"And why do you think me seeing him will
help the situation?" Thayer asked.

"Your father was his friend," replied the
doctor. "A young person like yourself might
be able to draw him out and get him to talk—
something I haven't been able to do."

"All right," said Thayer. "I'll give it a try."

When Thayer knocked on the door of the
doctor's cabin there was no answer. He took a
deep breath and went in. Ismay, still dressed in

his pajamas, was seated on his bunk, staring straight ahead. *He's shaking all over like a leaf,* Thayer thought.

The young man tried to start a conversation, but Ismay refused to talk. Thayer told him that there was no shame in what he did, that other men would have climbed into a lifeboat if they had been given the chance. Ismay said nothing.

It was then that Thayer noticed with a shock that the older man's hair had turned almost completely white. Finally, he left. As he closed the door he glanced back to see Ismay, still staring fixedly ahead.

Margaret Brown
The *Carpathia*'s dining saloon, 3:00 p.m.

Margaret Brown felt invigorated as she moved about the *Carpathia*, pouring her energy into several new projects. Using her knowledge of German, French, and Italian, she was able to communicate with and offer comfort to many third-class, non-English-speaking survivors.

Earlier in the day, Brown spoke to other first-class ladies about taking up a collection for the more unfortunate survivors who had lost everything when the *Titanic* sank. Some of them didn't express much interest, but Brown went ahead and scheduled a meeting that afternoon in the dining saloon.

Now a group of survivors from first and second class were gathered, at Brown's request, in the saloon. After a brief meeting, they voted to establish a survivors' committee with Brown as its chairwoman. Members committed $4,000 to the fund for the needy on board. Brown immediately began planning a strategy to grow the fund significantly in time for their arrival in New York in a few days.

Arthur Rostron

April 18, 1912, New York Harbor, 9:15 p.m.

It was a rainy night when Captain Rostron guided the *Carpathia* into New York. He was surprised but pleased to see thousands of people waiting at the docks despite the bad weather. He assumed they had come to welcome his ship and catch a glimpse of the survivors. There was good reason for their curiosity. Rostron had sent no details of the disaster on the ship's radio. He had reserved it only for essential traffic information and survivors sending messages to family.

From the bridge, Rostron watched the survivors depart his ship. They were worn and tired, many grieving lost husbands, sons, and other loved ones. But, at the same time, they seemed grateful to be alive. He felt sure that each of them, like himself, would never forget this experience. At the very least, he hoped they would all be better human beings for having lived through it.

EPILOGUE

The sinking of the *Titanic* captured the world's imagination in a way rivaled by few other disasters. More than 1,500 people died that terrible night in the North Atlantic, while only about 705 passengers and crew members survived. The event remains one of the worst tragedies in maritime history.

From the night they arrived in New York, survivors began to tell their stories of what happened. And these compelling stories of heroism and cowardice have been told and repeated in countless books, films, television programs, and even a Broadway musical.

The *Titanic*, the largest and most luxurious passenger ship of its time, has come to represent the folly of human technology. That a single encounter with an iceberg sank the supposedly "unsinkable" *Titanic* stunned people everywhere. To many, the tragedy served as a lesson in human overconfidence in the powers of science, technology, and authority.

In his book *The Sinking of the Titanic*, published the same year as the disaster, Logan Marshall wrote, "It [the sinking of the *Titanic*] was a symposium of horror and heroism, the like of which has not been known in the civilized world since man established his dominion over the sea."

John Jacob Astor IV may have died when one of the *Titanic*'s falling funnels crushed him as he was attempting to swim away from the ship. His body was later recovered from the sea. He was identified by the initials "J. J. A." on his shirt collar. A diamond studded watch hung from his pocket. It had stopped at 3:20 a.m.

Stories have been passed down, none of them verified, of heroic actions taken by Astor during the chaos. The most famous is how he helped a 10-year-old boy get aboard one of the last lifeboats. According to the story, Astor put a girl's hat on the boy and said, "Now he's a girl and he can go."

Captain Edward Smith's final moments also remain a mystery. Jack Thayer claimed to have seen Smith leap from the *Titanic*'s bridge just before it sank. Cook Isaac Maynard claimed he saw Smith swimming alongside his lifeboat just before the *Titanic* went down. Maynard said that Smith was pulled aboard but deliberately slipped back into the water saying, "I will follow the ship!"

Captain Arthur Rostron had a distinguished career as a sea captain and eventually became commodore of the Cunard Line. Among the many honors he received for his bold rescue of the *Titanic* survivors was the Congressional Gold Medal, given to him by U.S. President William Howard Taft. Rostron retired in 1931 and published a memoir, *Home From the Sea.* He died of pneumonia in 1940 at age 71.

Captain Stanley Lord was blamed by the public and the press for not aiding the *Titanic.* He was asked to resign his command, but was hired in 1913 by another steamship company. He retired in 1927 due to poor eyesight. The book *A Night to Remember* (1955) and the film based on it renewed the charge that Lord had sat idly by while the *Titanic* sank. He complained about the accusations to the Mercantile Marine Service Association, which defended him. He died on January 24, 1962, at age 84.

Leah Aks and her son were reunited in New York with her husband, Samuel. She was so grateful to Captain Rostron for restoring Filly to her that when she gave birth to a daughter the following year, she named the baby Sarah Carpathia Aks. However, the child's name was mistakenly recorded on the birth certificate as Sarah Titanic Aks. Leah Aks died in Norfolk on June 22, 1967.

Madeleine Astor gave birth to a son, John Jacob Astor V, four months after the *Titanic* disaster. During World War I, she married William Dick, an official for several companies. They divorced in 1933 and she married for a third time to prizefighter Enzo Fiermonte. They divorced in 1938. Madeleine Astor died in 1940 at age 47 in Palm Beach, Florida. John Jacob Astor V died in 1992 at age 79.

Lawrence Beesley wrote *The Loss of the SS* Titanic shortly after the disaster. It became a best seller. He returned to England, where the widower married for a second time and resumed his teaching career. He died on February 14, 1967, at age 89.

Harold Bride was met at New York Harbor by the inventor and wireless radio pioneer, Guglielmo

Marconi, who wanted to congratulate him on his work. Marconi was accompanied by a reporter from the *New York Times* who, with Marconi's approval, offered Bride $1,000 for his story of the disaster.

Bride returned to his native Great Britain and resumed his career as a radio operator. He married in 1919 and had three children. Uncomfortable with his fame as a *Titanic* survivor and disturbed by memories of that fateful night, Bride moved to rural Scotland with his family. He worked there as a traveling salesman. He died on April 29, 1956, at age 66.

Margaret Brown continued to work on behalf of the *Titanic* survivors. Soon after their return to New York, she presented a silver cup to Captain Rostron and medals to his crew for their valiant rescue efforts. For her many good acts, Brown received the French Legion of Honor in 1932. She died in New York on October 26, 1932, at the age of 65.

J. Bruce Ismay was criticized by the public and called a coward for surviving the disaster. The press labeled him J. "Brute" Ismay. People in the town of Ismay, Texas, considered changing the town's name to "Lowe" after Officer Harold Lowe, one of the heroes among the survivors. A broken man, Ismay resigned as director of the White Star Line within a year and moved to an estate on the west coast of Ireland. He lived there as a recluse until his death in 1937 at the age of 74.

Charles Joughin went on to work on many passenger ships. Years later he served on troop transport ships in World War II and retired in 1944. He died in New Jersey on December 9, 1956, at age 78.

Fifth Officer Harold Lowe returned to sea in the merchant service. He was made a commander in the Royal Naval Reserve in World War I. Lowe moved back to his native North Wales with his wife, Marion, and died there on May 12, 1944, at age 61.

Jack Thayer entered the University of Pennsylvania and, after graduating, went into banking. He married and had two sons. In 1940 he wrote a pamphlet about his experiences on the *Titanic*. One of his sons died serving in the Pacific during World War II. Depressed by the loss, Thayer took his own life in 1945 at age 50.

TIMELINE

10:55 P.M.: The *Californian* sends a warning message to the *Titanic* about icebergs nearby. The message is ignored.

11:40 P.M.: The *Titanic* strikes an iceberg, fatally damaging the ship.

APRIL 15, 1912

12:05 A.M.: Captain Edward Smith gives the order to his crew to alert the passengers and break out the lifeboats.

12:25 A.M.: The *Carpathia* receives the *Titanic's* distress message and turns around to help in the rescue effort.

12:45 A.M.: The first lifeboat, No. 7, containing 28 passengers, is lowered to the water. *Titanic* crew members start to send up distress rockets to get the attention of the *Californian*, only five miles away.

1:25 A.M.: Lifeboat No. 14, commanded by Fifth Officer Harold Lowe, is launched.

1:35 A.M.: Third-class passenger Leah Aks' baby is taken from her by a distraught man who hurls the infant overboard.

1:38 A.M.: J. Bruce Ismay, director of the White Star Line, climbs into Collapsible Boat C, one of the last to leave the ship.

1:45 A.M.: Lifeboat No. 4, the last of the regular lifeboats, is launched. On board are Madeleine Astor and Marian Thayer.

1:50 A.M.: Chief Baker Charles Joughin tosses deck chairs into the water as life preservers for the passengers who have jumped from the sinking ship.

2:05 A.M.: Captain Smith tells Jack Phillips and Harold Bride that they are released from duty.

2:10 A.M.: Jack Thayer and Milton Long decide to jump from the ship before it goes down.

2:15 A.M.: Jack Phillips is attacked by a stoker who tries to take his life belt. Bride comes to his aid and the two knock the attacker unconscious and then run from the radio cabin.

2:17 A.M.: A group of men, including Harold Bride, release the two remaining collapsible lifeboats. A wave, tumbling over the ship, washes both boats overboard.

2:20 A.M.: The *Titanic* sinks with more than a thousand people still aboard.

2:32 A.M.: Officer Lowe organizes several of the lifeboats and moves people among them.

2:35 A.M.: Officer Lightoller takes command of Collapsible B, which has flipped over in the water.

3:00 A.M.: Lowe takes his lifeboat back to the wreckage site in search of survivors. He finds only three people still alive.

4:00 A.M.: Joughin, who has been swimming for nearly two hours, is towed by Collapsible B. The *Carpathia* arrives at the site where the *Titanic* sank and crew members see the lifeboats.

4:10 A.M.: The first survivors, from Lifeboat No. 4, come aboard the *Carpathia*.

8:30 A.M.: The last of the lifeboats uploads its passengers on the *Carpathia*.

9:00 A.M.: The *Californian*, in communication with the *Carpathia*, searches for survivors in the water. Finding none, it continues on to Boston, Massachusetts.

April 16, 1912

3:00 P.M.: A group of passengers, led by Margaret Brown, form a survivors' committee to raise money for those who lost everything on the *Titanic*.

April 18, 1912

9:15 P.M.: The *Carpathia* arrives in New York Harbor with about 705 *Titanic* survivors.

GLOSSARY

bridge (BRIJ)—a platform on a ship from which the captain or pilot navigates

hypothermia (hi-puh-THUR-mee-uh)—a subnormal body temperature that can lead to illness or death

port (PORT)—the left-hand side of a ship or boat

premonition (pre-muh-NISH-uhn)—a feeling of anxiousness over a future event

purser (PUR-suhr)—a ship's officer in charge of documents and passengers' valuables

semaphore (SEM-uh-for)—a system of signals from ship to ship using lights or flags

starboard (STAR-buhrd)—the right-hand side of a ship or boat

stern (STURN)—the back or rear part of a vessel

stoker (STO-kuhr)—a worker who tends to and fuels a furnace to create steam on a steamship

suffrage (SUF-rij)—the right to vote

CRITICAL THINKING USING THE COMMON CORE

1. The *Titanic* tragedy was the result of a series of errors, any one of which, if corrected, could have prevented the ship's sinking or at least saved the lives of many more people. Name some of them and explain how each error could have been corrected. (Key Ideas and Details)

2. Historians point to the *Titanic* disaster as a turning point in modern history. Before, people had faith in technology and authority. Why do you think these attitudes changed? What major event soon followed the sinking of the *Titanic* that further changed the world? Refer to the text and outside sources for your answer. (Integration of Knowledge and Ideas)

3. Surprisingly, some good came out of the terrible tragedy of the *Titanic*. The number of lifeboats on ocean-going ships was increased to provide for all people aboard. Monitoring of icebergs in the North Atlantic became an annual event. And in 1913, the first Safety of Life at Sea Convention was convened. Research one or more of these changes and show how the *Titanic* disaster led directly to its adoption. (Integration of Knowledge and Ideas)

INTERNET SITES

FactHound offers a safe, fun way to find Internet sites related to this book. All of the sites on FactHound have been researched by our staff.

Here's all you do:
Visit www.facthound.com
Type in this code: 9781491484531

FactHound will fetch the best sites for you!

FURTHER READING

Dougherty, Terri. *The Titanic's Crew: Working Aboard the Great Ship*. North Mankato, Minn.: Capstone Press, 2015.

Lassieur, Allison. *Can You Survive the* Titanic?: *An Interactive Survival Adventure*. Mankato, Minn.: Capstone Press, 2012.

Stewart, Melissa. Titanic. Washington, D.C.: National Geographic, 2012.

Tarshis, Lauren. *I Survived the Sinking of the* Titanic, *1912*. New York: Scholastic, 2010.

SELECTED BIBLIOGRAPHY

Barczewski, Stephanie. Titanic: *A Night Remembered.* New York: Hambledon Continuum, 2006.

Brewster, Hugh. *Gilded Lives, Fatal Voyage: The* Titanic, *Her Passengers and Their World.* New York: Crown, 2011.

Davenport-Hines, Richard. *Voyagers of the* Titanic: *Passengers, Sailors, Shipbuilders, Aristocrats, and the Worlds They Came From.* New York: William Morrow, 2012.

Davie, Michael. Titanic: *The Death and Life of a Legend.* New York: Vintage Books, a division of Random House, Inc., 2012.

Everett, Marshall. *Wreck and Sinking of the* Titanic. New York: Harper Design, an imprint of HarperCollins Publishers, 2011.

Lord, Walter. *A Night to Remember.* Lodi, N.J.: Everbind Anthologies, 2010.

Maltin, Tim. *101 Things You Thought You Knew About the* Titanic— *But Didn't!* New York: Penguin Books, 2011.

Maltin, Tim, ed. Titanic, *First Accounts.* New York: Penguin Classics, 2012.

Wilson, Andrew. *Shadow of the* Titanic: *The Extraordinary Stories of Those Who Survived.* New York: Atria Books, 2012.

Winocour, Jack, ed. *The Story of the* Titanic, *As Told by Its Survivors.* New York: Dover, 1960.

INDEX

ABOUT THE AUTHOR

Steven Otfinoski has written more than 170 books for young readers. His previous book in the Tangled History series is *Day of Infamy*. Among his many other books for Capstone is the You Choose book *The Sinking of the Lusitania*. Three of his nonfiction books have been named Books for the Teen Age by the New York Public Library. He lives in Connecticut with his family.